CLARA BARTON

BOOK FOR CURIOUS KIDS

The Inspiring Legacy of the Angel of the Battlefield and Founder of the American Red Cross

ERIC LYLANI

ERIC LYLANI

TABLE OF CONTENTS

INTRODUCTION

Have you ever wondered what drives someone to dedicate their life to helping others? What inspires a person to stand up for education, care for the wounded, and pioneer humanitarian efforts across continents?

Join me on a journey into the extraordinary life of Clara Barton—a woman whose courage, compassion, and unwavering dedication reshaped the landscape of education and humanitarian aid. In the pages ahead, we'll unravel the gripping saga of Clara Barton, from her humble beginnings to her pivotal role as the founder of the American Red Cross.

How did Clara's early experiences shape her destiny? What led her to become known as the "Angel of the Battlefield"? And what enduring legacy did she leave for future generations?

Buckle up as we delve into Clara's captivating story, from her relentless pursuit of education to her fearless journeys on the front lines of history. Discover the profound impact of one woman's unwavering resolve to make a difference in the world.

Are you ready to uncover Clara Barton's remarkable saga and timeless lessons of compassion and resilience? Let's embark on this inspiring adventure together.

Early Days

Once upon a time, in a small town called North Oxford, Massachusetts, there was a little girl named Clarissa Harlowe Barton. She was born on a special day—December 25, 1821—right on Christmas Day! Clara, as everyone called her, came into the world full of curiosity and wonder.

Clara's parents were Captain Stephen Barton and Sarah Stone Barton. Her father was a brave member of the local militia, which is like a group of volunteers who help protect their community. Captain Barton was also a selectman, which meant he was involved in making important decisions for their town. He loved his country dearly, and his strong sense of patriotism and kindness influenced Clara a lot as she grew up.

But Captain Barton's life wasn't just about local politics. He had also been a soldier under General Anthony Wayne during a difficult time in history. He fought in wars that were part of America's westward expansion, which often involved conflicts with Indigenous peoples. This was a challenging and important part of Clara's family story, showing both the bravery and complexity of her father's life.

Clara's mother, Sarah Stone Barton, played an essential role in Clara's upbringing, too. She taught Clara about compassion and caring for others. Together, Clara's parents created a loving home where Clara and her siblings could learn and grow.

When Clara was around three years old, she started going to school with her older brother, Stephen. At school, Clara discovered a love for reading and learning. She excelled at reading books and spelling words. Despite being a bit shy and timid, Clara made her first close friend at school, a girl named Nancy Fitts. Nancy became Clara's best friend and companion during their early school days.

As Clara grew, she listened eagerly to her father's stories about history and bravery. She admired her father's dedication to helping others and learned from his strong sense of duty and service. Clara's mother, Sarah, taught her the importance of kindness and empathy towards everyone, regardless of their background or circumstances.

In the peaceful town of North Oxford, young Clara Barton's heart was filled with dreams of making a difference in the world. Little did she know that her adventurous spirit and compassionate nature would lead her on a remarkable journey—one that would inspire countless lives and change the course of history forever.

Clara's childhood was filled with love, learning, and the seeds of her future calling. Her experiences in North Oxford shaped her into the brave and caring woman who would one day become known as the "Angel of the Battlefield." But for now, she was just a curious girl with big dreams and a heart full of hope.

Healing Touch

When Clara Barton was ten years old, something happened that would change her life forever. Her brother David fell from the roof of a barn and hurt his head very badly. Clara knew she had to help. For two whole years, Clara became David's nurse, taking care of him every day.

Clara learned a lot during those years of caring for her brother. She discovered how to give him the medicine he needed to feel better. Sometimes, she even had to perform a practice called bloodletting. This meant using leeches to remove blood from her brother's body to help him heal. It was a strange and tricky job, but Clara did it with courage and love for her brother.

Day by day, Clara saw her brother get stronger and healthier. Her care and determination paid off when David eventually made a full recovery. Clara felt a deep sense of happiness and accomplishment, knowing she had helped save her brother's life.

However, being a nurse at such a young age was not easy for Clara. She was naturally shy and quiet, and taking care of her brother through such a serious injury was overwhelming. Instead of feeling proud, Clara started to feel more timid and sad. She became so worried that she stopped eating properly.

In an effort to help Clara become more outgoing and happy, her parents decided to send her to Colonel Stones High School. They hoped that being around other children and learning new things would bring back Clara's joy. But being away from home and facing new challenges made Clara even more anxious and unhappy.

Clara missed her family dearly and found it hard to adjust to school life. She felt lost and out of place in the bustling hallways and classrooms. Her sadness grew, and she struggled to find her place among her peers.

Seeing their daughter's distress, Clara's parents made the difficult decision to bring her back home. They knew that Clara's health and happiness were more important than anything else. Back in the comfort of her own home, Clara slowly regained her strength and spirit.

During this time, Clara discovered a new sense of purpose. Caring for her brother had taught her the power of compassion and perseverance. Though she was still young and unsure of herself, Clara's experiences would soon lead her on a remarkable journey—one that would show the world just how brave and capable she truly was.

Embarking on the Path of Teaching

After returning home and recovering from her struggles at school, Clara Barton's life took another turn. Her family decided to move to help a widowed cousin manage her farm and children. This cousin needed all the help she could get after her husband passed away, leaving her with four children and a farm to look after.

Clara wasn't one to shy away from hard work. She jumped right in, assisting with repairs and maintenance around the new home where her family would live. Clara showed her strength and determination as she helped make the house a comfortable place for her family and her cousin's family to live.

Despite her hard work, Clara worried about being a burden to her family. She wanted to contribute and be helpful in every way she could. To keep busy and fit in with her cousins, Clara joined them in activities like horseback riding. She loved the thrill of riding through fields and forests, feeling the wind in her hair.

However, one day, Clara had an accident while riding. Concerned for her safety, her mother decided it was time for Clara to focus on learning more "traditionally feminine" skills. She invited a female cousin to help Clara develop these skills, such as sewing, cooking, and other household tasks.

As Clara grew older, her parents saw that she was still struggling with shyness and timidity. They believed that becoming a schoolteacher might help Clara overcome her fears and gain confidence. With their encouragement, Clara enrolled at the Clinton Liberal Institute in Clinton, New York.

At just seventeen years old, Clara achieved her first teacher's certificate. She was now ready to embark on a new adventure— teaching young children. Clara was determined to make a difference in the lives of her students, just as she had done for her brother and her family.

One of Clara's first challenges as a teacher was to campaign for better education opportunities for all children. She led a successful campaign to rearrange school districts, ensuring that even children of workers had access to education. Clara's efforts showed her passion for equality and fairness, traits that would define her future endeavors.

Educational Pursuits

Clara Barton's journey as a teacher began in 1838, and for the next eleven years, she dedicated herself to educating children in and around her hometown of Oxford, Massachusetts. As a teacher, Clara discovered a deep passion for helping young minds grow and learn.

Clara's time as a teacher was filled with joy and challenges. She had a special talent for understanding children, especially the energetic boys in her classes. Growing up with boy cousins and brothers, Clara knew how to relate to them. She could act like one of the boys, which made it easier for her to connect with and guide them in their studies.

Clara's classrooms were lively places where learning was fun. She used her creativity and enthusiasm to make lessons exciting and engaging. Whether teaching reading, writing, or arithmetic, Clara always found a way to capture her students' attention and inspire them to excel.

In 1851, Clara faced a heartbreaking loss when her mother passed away. With the family home closing down, Clara realized it was time for a new chapter in her life. She made a bold decision to further her education by attending the Clinton Liberal Institute in New York.

At the institute, Clara immersed herself in the world of writing and languages. She eagerly embraced new subjects and ideas, expanding her horizons and deepening her understanding of the world. Clara made many friends at the institute, and these friendships broadened her perspective on important issues of the time.

Clara's talent as a writer shone brightly during her time at the institute. Her writing was clear, precise, and easy to understand—qualities that made her work stand out. Clara's writings were not just admired for their quality; they also had the power to educate and inspire local leaders and statesmen.

ERIC LYLANI

Championing Education

As Clara Barton continued her teaching journey, she encountered a new challenge that would ignite her passion for education and equality. While teaching in Hightstown, New Jersey, Clara discovered that the neighboring city of Bordentown had no public schools for children who couldn't afford to pay. This troubled Clara deeply.

In 1852, Clara was offered a special opportunity—to open the very first free school in New Jersey, right in Bordentown! Clara eagerly accepted the contract and set out to make a difference.

Opening the free school was no easy task, but Clara was determined to succeed. She worked tirelessly, teaching and inspiring over 600 students. To help manage such a large class, Clara hired another woman to assist her. Together, they brought education to children who otherwise might not have had the chance to learn.

Clara's success did not go unnoticed. The town was so impressed by her dedication and the impact of the free school that they raised nearly $4,000 to build a brand-new school building. It was a proud moment for Clara, knowing that her efforts had sparked such positive change in the community.

However, not everyone was supportive of Clara's leadership. Despite her achievements, the school board believed that a woman should not hold such a prominent position. Clara was replaced as principal by a man chosen by the school board simply because they thought a woman wasn't suitable to lead a large institution.

Demoted to the role of "female assistant," Clara faced a difficult and unfair situation. The environment became harsh, and the stress took a toll on her health. Clara experienced a nervous breakdown and other health issues, which ultimately led her to resign from her position.

Though Clara's time in Bordentown ended with challenges, her determination and courage never wavered. She had fought for the right of every child to receive an education, regardless of their background or circumstances. Clara's experience fueled her passion for equality and justice, shaping her future path in extraordinary ways.

ERIC LYLANI

Courageous Advocacy

In 1855, Clara Barton embarked on a new chapter of her life by moving to Washington, D.C. She started working as a clerk in the U.S. Patent Office—an important job that marked a historic milestone. Clara was the first woman to hold such a significant position in the federal government, earning a salary equal to that of a man. This was a remarkable achievement!

However, Clara faced many challenges in her new role. The male clerks at the Patent Office were not used to working alongside a woman in such a respected position. They treated Clara with disrespect and unkindness, subjecting her to abuse and slander. Despite these hardships, Clara remained determined and focused on proving herself through hard work and dedication.

Unfortunately, political opposition to women working in government offices soon threatened Clara's position. Her role was downgraded to that of a copyist—a less prestigious job—due to discriminatory views against women in the workplace.

In 1858, during James Buchanan's presidency, Clara was unfairly dismissed from her job because of her political beliefs. She was labeled a "Black Republican" due to her support for the anti-slavery Republican Party. It was a difficult time for Clara, facing discrimination and losing her livelihood because of her principles.

After three years of living with relatives and friends in Massachusetts, Clara returned to the U.S. Patent Office in 1860. She accepted a temporary role as a copyist, hoping to pave the way for more women to join government service. Clara's determination to challenge gender barriers and fight for equality was stronger than ever.

Clara Barton's journey in Washington, D.C., was marked by resilience and bravery. Despite facing prejudice and adversity, she refused to give up on her dreams of equality and opportunity for all. Clara's experiences taught her the importance of standing up for what she believed in, even when faced with opposition.

ERIC LYLANI

The Beginning of a Heroic Journey

On a fateful day, April 19, 1861, the United States was thrust into the tumultuous period of the Civil War. The city of Baltimore erupted into violence during what became known as the Baltimore Riot—a tragic event that marked the beginning of this historic conflict.

Amidst the chaos and uncertainty, Clara Barton found herself at the heart of the unfolding drama. Living in Washington, D.C., at the time, Clara was deeply moved by the suffering of the wounded soldiers arriving from the riot. Determined to make a difference and serve her country, Clara rushed to the railroad station where the victims were being transported.

When Clara arrived at the station, she was faced with a scene of devastation. The soldiers, members of the 6th Massachusetts Militia, were wounded, hungry, and in desperate need of care. Many of them were her friends and former students whom she had known since childhood.

Without hesitation, Clara Barton sprang into action. Drawing on her experiences as a nurse and educator, Clara provided vital assistance to the soldiers. She brought food, clothing, and medical supplies to comfort and support the brave men in uniform.

Clara's compassion and dedication knew no bounds. She personally tended to the soldiers, offering not just physical aid but also emotional support. Clara understood the importance of lifting their spirits during such a challenging time. She read books to them, wrote letters to their families on their behalf, and simply listened to their stories and worries.

As Clara cared for the soldiers, she learned valuable lessons in storing and distributing medical supplies—a skill that would prove crucial in the days to come. Her selflessness and tireless efforts earned her the admiration and gratitude of those she served.

Clara Barton's involvement in the aftermath of the Baltimore Riot marked the beginning of her extraordinary journey as a humanitarian. She had found her calling—to be a beacon of hope and healing for those in need during one of the darkest periods in American history.

Dedication to Soldiers' Welfare

After witnessing the harrowing aftermath of the Baltimore Riot, Clara Barton's heart was stirred with a newfound purpose—to serve and support the brave soldiers fighting in the Civil War. It was a day that would change her life forever.

Inspired by her experience at the railroad station, Clara identified herself with army work and made it her mission to collect essential medical supplies for the Union soldiers. Despite facing opposition and challenges, Clara was determined to make a difference.

In early 1862, Clara transformed her own living quarters into a storeroom for provisions. With the help of a few devoted friends, she began distributing supplies to the soldiers. The War Department and field surgeons initially resisted Clara's efforts, but she remained undeterred.

The Ladies' Aid Society played a crucial role in supporting Clara's mission. They sent much-needed bandages, food, and clothing that would later be distributed directly to soldiers on the battlefield. Clara's determination and resourcefulness were evident as she navigated the obstacles in her path.

In August 1862, after persistent efforts, Clara Barton finally gained permission from Quartermaster Daniel Rucker to work on the front lines. This was a significant milestone that allowed Clara to directly aid and comfort wounded soldiers in the midst of battle.

Supported by dedicated patrons like Senator Henry Wilson of Massachusetts, Clara Barton's impact grew. She placed advertisements in newspapers for supplies and received an overwhelming response from generous donors across the country.

Clara Barton's work took her to the heart of the war's most brutal battles. From Cedar Mountain to Antietam and Fredericksburg, Clara fearlessly ventured to aid soldiers on both sides—Union and Confederate. She did not discriminate; her mission was to provide care and comfort to all who needed it.

Supplies were often scarce, but Clara's ingenuity knew no bounds. At the battle of Antietam, when bandages ran out, Clara improvised with corn husks to tend to the wounded. Her resourcefulness and resilience saved countless lives in desperate circumstances.

Clara Barton's commitment to her role as a nurse was unwavering. She faced danger without fear, knowing that her place was by the side of the soldiers, providing not just medical aid but also emotional support and encouragement.

In Clara's own words, "I shall remain here while anyone remains, and do whatever comes to my hand." Her selfless dedication and courage in the face of adversity inspired all who knew her. Clara Barton had become a beacon of hope and compassion amid the chaos of war—a true hero whose legacy would endure for generations to come.

Journey to Port Royal

In April 1863, Clara Barton embarked on another extraordinary adventure, accompanying her brother David to Port Royal, South Carolina. David had been appointed as a quartermaster in the Union Navy, and Clara eagerly joined him in the Union-occupied Sea Islands.

Settling into life on the Sea Islands, Clara Barton quickly found herself immersed in a community dedicated to supporting and educating formerly enslaved people. Here, she formed friendships with notable abolitionists and feminists like Frances Dana Barker Gage, who had come to the South to provide education and empowerment to those who had recently gained their freedom.

During her time in South Carolina, Clara also met Jean Margaret Davenport, an English actress residing on the Sea Islands with her husband, Union General Frederick W. Lander. The Sea Islands were teeming with vibrant personalities and important figures, all united in the cause of freedom and justice.

Clara Barton's compassion and dedication to nursing extended to all soldiers, regardless of their background. She provided vital medical care to the Black soldiers of the 54th Massachusetts Regiment after their valiant attack on Fort Wagner. Clara's presence brought comfort and healing to these brave men.

In addition to her work on the Sea Islands, Clara traveled to Morris Island to tend to Union soldiers stationed there. She was accompanied by Betsey, a Black woman who worked under Clara's guidance during her time in South Carolina. Together, they provided essential care and support to the soldiers.

Clara's commitment to her work sometimes led to disagreements with military leaders. She clashed with General Quincy Adams Gillmore after he abruptly ordered her to leave her post at Morris Island. Clara's determination to serve the soldiers often put her at odds with those who underestimated her abilities and dedication.

Clara Barton's experiences in Port Royal were marked by courage, compassion, and resilience. Her dedication to serving humanity, regardless of race or status, exemplifies the spirit of kindness and equality that defined her remarkable life. Clara's journey was far from over, and greater challenges and triumphs awaited her in the days ahead.

Angel of the Battlefield

In 1864, Clara Barton's dedication and bravery led to her appointment by Union General Benjamin Butler as the "lady in charge" of hospitals at the front lines of the Army of the James. This marked a significant moment in Clara's journey—a recognition of her tireless efforts and unwavering commitment to caring for the wounded soldiers.

Clara Barton's experiences on the battlefield were filled with both courage and heartbreak. During one harrowing incident, a bullet tore through the sleeve of her dress, narrowly missing her, and tragically struck a man she was tending to.

Despite the dangers, Clara remained steadfast in her mission to bring comfort and healing to those in need.

Clara Barton's compassion and selflessness earned her the nickname "Florence Nightingale of America." Like Florence Nightingale, Clara became a symbol of hope and compassion during times of war, bringing light to the darkest of moments.

Another title bestowed upon Clara was the "Angel of the Battlefield." This name reflected her remarkable acts of heroism and kindness as she rushed to aid overwhelmed surgeons and care for severely wounded soldiers on numerous battlefields.

After the battle of Cedar Mountain in Northern Virginia, Clara's timely assistance at field hospitals became legendary. She arrived at midnight with a vast supply of essential items to help ease the suffering of the soldiers. Her presence and dedication made a profound difference in the lives of those she cared for.

Clara Barton's angelic presence was felt at many crucial battles, including Fairfax Station, Chantilly, Harpers Ferry, South Mountain, Antietam, Fredericksburg, Charleston, Petersburg, and Cold Harbor. Wherever there was suffering and need, Clara Barton was there, offering comfort, support, and practical assistance.

Clara's unwavering commitment to the soldiers transcended fear and danger. She never hesitated to face the perils of the battlefield if it meant she could provide aid and solace to those in distress.

In Clara's own words, "I may be compelled to face danger, but never fear it." Her courage and resilience inspired all who crossed her path, leaving an indelible mark on the hearts of those she served.

Mission: Finding the Missing Soldiers

After the American Civil War ended, Clara Barton discovered a heartbreaking truth—thousands of letters from worried families to the War Department were left unanswered because their loved ones were buried in unmarked graves. Many soldiers were listed as "missing," leaving families in anguish and uncertainty.

Motivated by compassion and a desire to help, Clara Barton took action. She reached out to President Lincoln, seeking permission to respond to these unanswered inquiries officially. President Lincoln recognized

Clara's dedication and granted her permission to start what would become known as "The Search for the Missing Men."

Setting up the Office of Missing Soldiers at 437 $\frac{1}{2}$ Seventh Street, Northwest, in Washington, D.C., Clara Barton and her team embarked on a monumental mission—to find and identify soldiers who were killed or missing during the war.

Day after day, Clara and her assistants tirelessly worked to answer inquiries and locate missing soldiers. They wrote over 41,000 replies to worried families, bringing much-needed closure and comfort to thousands of homes across the nation.

One of Clara's most significant tasks was helping to locate and properly bury those who perished in the brutal conditions of the

Andersonville prison camp in Georgia. In the summer of 1865, Clara spent months searching for, identifying, and respectfully burying 13,000 individuals who had died in the camp.

But Clara's mission did not end there. Over the next four years, she continued her efforts, burying another 20,000 Union soldiers and ensuring that each grave was marked with dignity and honor.

Clara Barton's dedication caught the attention of Congress, which recognized the importance of her work. Congress eventually appropriated $15,000 to support Clara's project, underscoring the significance of her efforts in bringing closure to families and honoring the memory of fallen soldiers.

Clara Barton's work in finding and honoring the missing soldiers became a powerful symbol of compassion and dedication. Her unwavering commitment to serving others, even after the war had ended, reflected her belief in the importance of bringing comfort and closure to those who had sacrificed so much.

Clara Barton's legacy as a humanitarian and advocate for the fallen soldiers lives on, reminding us of the profound impact one person can make in times of great need. Her story inspires us all to reach out with kindness and empathy, making a difference in the lives of others.

Global Humanitarian Endeavors

After years of dedicated service following the Civil War, Clara Barton found herself thrust into the spotlight for her remarkable experiences. From 1865 to 1868, Clara traveled across the country, sharing her stories and insights from the war in lectures that captivated audiences everywhere.

During her travels, Clara Barton crossed paths with influential figures like Susan B. Anthony, a leading advocate for women's suffrage, and Frederick Douglass, a prominent leader in the fight for civil rights. Inspired by these encounters, Clara became an outspoken activist for both women's rights and civil liberties.

Despite her growing recognition, Clara Barton faced challenges. The demanding nature of her work took a toll on her health, leaving her mentally and physically exhausted. Under doctor's orders, Clara sought respite far from her daily responsibilities.

In 1868, Clara made the difficult decision to close the Missing Soldiers Office and embark on a journey to Europe in search of healing and renewal. Little did she know that her travels would lead to a pivotal encounter that would change her life forever.

During her stay in Geneva, Switzerland, Clara Barton was introduced to the Red Cross and its visionary founder, Dr. Appia.

Dr. Appia recognized Clara's passion for humanitarian work and invited her to become the representative for the American branch of the Red Cross.

The concept of the Red Cross, inspired by Henry Dunant's book "A Memory of Solferino," deeply resonated with Clara Barton. Dunant's book advocated for the formation of national societies to provide relief voluntarily on a neutral basis, a vision that aligned perfectly with Clara's own values and beliefs.

Clara Barton's encounter with the Red Cross ignited a new mission within her—to establish the American Red Cross and bring its lifesaving mission to the United States. Determined and inspired, Clara set out to find financial supporters who could help turn this vision into reality.

Clara Barton's journey in Europe was a transformative period of discovery and purpose. Her passion for humanitarian work, coupled with her unwavering commitment to serving others, laid the groundwork for her most significant endeavor yet—the establishment of the American Red Cross.

As Clara Barton embarked on this new chapter, she carried with her the lessons and experiences that had shaped her into a fearless advocate for humanity. Her journey was far from over, and her impact would continue to resonate around the world, leaving an enduring legacy of compassion and courage.

Pioneering the Red Cross Movement

As the Franco-Prussian War loomed in 1870, Clara Barton's unwavering dedication to humanitarian efforts led her to assist the Grand Duchess of Baden in preparing military hospitals and providing vital aid through the Red Cross society during the conflict. Clara's selfless actions earned her admiration and gratitude from those she served.

During the Siege of Paris in 1871, Clara Barton's compassion knew no bounds. At the request of German authorities and the Strasbourg Comité de Secours, Clara supervised the distribution of work to the impoverished people of Strasbourg, ensuring that they received essential support during this challenging time.

After the war, Clara Barton's humanitarian efforts extended to Paris, where she took charge of distributing supplies to the destitute population. Her tireless commitment to helping those in need earned her prestigious honors, including the Golden Cross of Baden and the Prussian Iron Cross—testaments to her extraordinary service and dedication.

Upon her return to the United States, Clara Barton embarked on a new mission—to gain recognition for the International Committee of the Red Cross (ICRC) by the U.S. government. In 1873, Clara Barton began her tireless advocacy efforts to secure official support for the Red Cross.

Despite initial skepticism, Clara Barton's perseverance paid off. In 1878, she met with President Rutherford B. Hayes to champion the cause of the Red Cross. Although many believed that America would not face another crisis like the Civil War, Clara Barton argued that the Red Cross could play a crucial role in responding to natural disasters such as earthquakes, forest fires, and hurricanes.

Clara Barton's determined efforts finally bore fruit during President Chester Arthur's administration. She successfully persuaded the government to recognize and support the American Red Cross, paving the way for a new era of humanitarian relief in the United States.

In 1881, Clara Barton was appointed President of the American Red Cross, a momentous milestone that marked the official establishment of the society. The first official meeting of the American Red Cross took place at Clara Barton's apartment in Washington, D.C., on May 21, 1881.

Under Clara Barton's leadership, the American Red Cross quickly expanded its reach. The first local society was founded in Dansville, New York, in August 1881, demonstrating Clara's vision of creating a nationwide network of support and relief.

During the Spanish-American War, the American Red Cross played a crucial role in aiding refugees and prisoners of the civil conflict. Clara Barton's dedication earned her widespread recognition, including a statue erected in her honor by the grateful people of Santiago, a testament to her enduring impact and legacy.

Lifetime Commitment to Service

Throughout her life, Clara Barton's unwavering dedication to humanitarian causes continued to shine brightly, both within the United States and across the globe. From responding to domestic disasters to providing aid in international crises, Clara Barton's legacy of compassion knew no bounds.

In 1884, Clara Barton leaped into action during the devastating floods along the Ohio River. She rallied support and provided much-needed assistance to the affected communities, demonstrating her commitment to helping those in times of crisis.

Three years later, Texas faced a severe famine, and Clara Barton swiftly organized efforts to deliver food and supplies to the struggling population. Her leadership and compassion brought hope to countless families in their hour of need.

In 1888, a tornado ravaged Illinois, leaving destruction in its wake. Clara Barton wasted no time in mobilizing workers and resources to aid the affected communities, offering comfort and support to those who had lost everything.

That same year, Clara Barton responded to another crisis—the yellow fever epidemic in Florida. She assembled a team of dedicated workers and traveled to the affected areas, providing essential medical care and assistance to those suffering from the deadly disease.

In 1889, the devastating Johnstown Flood shook Pennsylvania. Within days, Clara Barton led a delegation of 50 doctors and nurses to respond to the disaster, laying the foundation for what would become the Conemaugh Health System—a testament to her quick action and organizational skills.

In 1896, Clara Barton embarked on an international mission of mercy to the Ottoman Empire, where she witnessed the aftermath of the Hamidian massacres. Barton and her team provided vital relief and humanitarian aid to the Armenian population, offering comfort and support to those affected by the atrocities.

Clara Barton's humanitarian efforts extended to Cuba in 1898, where she volunteered in hospitals despite being 77 years old. Her unwavering commitment to serving others knew no limits, inspiring all who crossed her path.

In 1900, Clara Barton's final field operation as President of the American Red Cross took her to Galveston, Texas, in the aftermath of a devastating hurricane. She spearheaded relief efforts and established an orphanage for children orphaned by the disaster, leaving a lasting impact on the community.

Clara Barton's life was a testament to the power of compassion and resilience. Her unwavering commitment to helping others, whether at home or abroad, continues to inspire generations to make a difference in the lives of those in need.

Enduring Impact and Legacy

In her later years, Clara Barton faced challenges and changes within the American Red Cross. Despite her lifelong dedication and achievements, criticism arose about her management style and the blending of personal and professional resources.

In 1904, at the age of 83, Clara Barton made the difficult decision to resign as President of the American Red Cross. This decision was influenced by pressure from a new generation of leaders, mostly male experts focused on efficiency and structure during the Progressive Era.

Clara Barton's departure from the American Red Cross marked the end of an era. Her idealistic vision clashed with the evolving landscape of organizational charity, prompting her to step aside and make room for new leadership.

However, Clara Barton's impact on the Red Cross was profound. In honor of the courageous women who served during the Civil War, the Red Cross Headquarters was founded. During the dedication ceremony, a poignant silence was observed—a powerful tribute to the women whose selfless service had paved the way for future humanitarian efforts.

After resigning from the American Red Cross, Clara Barton's spirit of service continued to guide her. She founded the National First Aid Society, recognizing the importance of emergency response and medical assistance in communities across the nation.

Clara Barton's enduring legacy extends far beyond her time as President of the American Red Cross. Her unwavering dedication to humanitarian causes, coupled with her fearless leadership and boundless compassion, inspired generations to follow in her footsteps.

Despite facing criticism and challenges, Clara Barton's impact on the world of humanitarian aid remains unparalleled. Her legacy lives on in the principles and values that continue to guide organizations like the American Red Cross, embodying the spirit of service and compassion that Clara Barton exemplified throughout her remarkable life.

ERIC LYLANI

Lasting Contributions

After resigning from the American Red Cross, Clara Barton continued to live in her beloved home in Glen Echo, Maryland. This historic house also served as the Red Cross Headquarters from the time she moved there in 1897. Despite stepping away from formal leadership roles, Clara Barton's dedication to humanitarian causes never wavered.

In 1908, at the age of 87, Clara Barton published her autobiography titled "The Story of My Childhood." Through her memoir, Clara Barton shared her remarkable life experiences, inspiring readers with tales of courage, compassion, and resilience.

As the years passed, Clara Barton's health began to decline. On April 12, 1912, at the age of 90, Clara Barton passed away peacefully in her home. The cause of her death was pneumonia.

Clara Barton's passing marked the end of an extraordinary life devoted to serving others. Her legacy as a trailblazer in humanitarian aid, emergency response, and advocacy for the vulnerable continues to inspire people around the world.

Throughout her long and remarkable life, Clara Barton touched countless lives and left an indelible imprint on history. Her unwavering commitment to compassion and service laid the groundwork for modern humanitarian organizations like the American Red Cross.

Today, Clara Barton is remembered not only for her groundbreaking work but also for her enduring spirit of resilience and determination. Her legacy serves as a beacon of hope and inspiration for generations, reminding us of the profound impact one person can make in the world.

Clara Barton's contributions to humanity live on through the enduring mission of the American Red Cross, which continues to provide lifesaving aid and assistance to those in need during times of crisis and disaster.

As we reflect on Clara Barton's remarkable journey, let us honor her memory by carrying forward her legacy of compassion, courage, and service. May her extraordinary life serve as a reminder that each of us has the power to make a difference and leave a lasting impact on the world around us.

Clara Barton's story is a testament to the transformative power of compassion and the enduring legacy of a life dedicated to serving others. Her memory lives on in the hearts of all who continue to be inspired by her remarkable example of selfless devotion and unwavering compassion.

Honoring Clara Barton's Legacy

In 1975, a special place was created to honor the incredible achievements of Clara Barton—the Clara Barton National Historic Site. Located at 5801 Oxford Road in Glen Echo, Maryland, this site preserves the home where Clara Barton spent the last 15 years of her remarkable life. It holds a special distinction as the first National Historic Site dedicated to the accomplishments of a woman.

Clara Barton's home not only served as her residence but also played a significant role in the early history of the American Red

Cross. It served as one of the organization's early headquarters, where Clara Barton tirelessly worked to provide aid and assistance to those in need.

The National Park Service took great care to restore eleven rooms within Clara Barton's home, including the Red Cross offices, parlors, and Barton's own bedroom. Visitors to the site had the unique opportunity to step back in time and gain insight into Clara Barton's life and work. Knowledgeable guides led tours through the three levels of the house, highlighting Clara Barton's use of her distinctive home as a base for her humanitarian efforts.

However, in October 2015, the site temporarily closed for repairs. Despite efforts to reopen, the closure was extended due to the COVID-19 pandemic, remaining shuttered through 2021. Fortunately, in 2022, the house reopened its doors to the public, albeit with some limitations. The second and third floors of the house remain closed due to structural concerns, but visitors can still explore the ground floor and learn about Clara Barton's incredible legacy.

Today, the Clara Barton National Historic Site stands as a testament to the enduring impact of one woman's dedication to service and compassion. It serves as a place of inspiration and education, allowing visitors to learn about Clara Barton's pioneering efforts in humanitarian aid and the early history of the American Red Cross.

As visitors walk through the restored rooms

of Clara Barton's home, they are transported back in time to an era of courage, resilience, and hope. Clara Barton's spirit lives on in the walls of her beloved home, reminding us all of the power of compassion and the difference one person can make in the world.

The Clara Barton National Historic Site is more than just a museum—it is a living tribute to the legacy of a remarkable woman who dedicated her life to helping others. It invites us to honor Clara Barton's memory and continue her work of spreading kindness, empathy, and assistance to those in need.

Rediscovering Clara Barton's Legacy

In 1869, after years of dedicated service in locating missing soldiers and helping families reunite, Clara Barton made the decision to close the Missing Soldiers Office. She then embarked on a new journey—to Europe, where she would continue her humanitarian work and advocacy.

Over time, the building that housed Clara Barton's Missing Soldiers Office fell into disuse and was eventually boarded up in 1913. The site faded from memory, obscured by changes in Washington, D.C.'s addressing system in the 1870s. What was once Clara

Barton's office became known as 437 $\frac{1}{2}$ Seventh Street Northwest (formerly 488-1/2 Seventh Street West), lost to the passage of time.

Fast forward to 1997, when a General Services Administration carpenter named Richard Lyons was tasked with inspecting the building for demolition. Little did he know he would stumble upon an incredible discovery—a hidden treasure trove of artifacts belonging to Clara Barton. In the attic, Richard Lyons found signs, clothing, Civil War-era items like soldier's socks and an army tent, old newspapers, and numerous documents related to the Office of Missing Soldiers.

This remarkable find sparked renewed interest in Clara Barton's legacy and led to the National Park Service stepping in to save the historic building from demolition.

However, it would take several years for the site to be fully restored and transformed into a museum worthy of Clara Barton's memory.

Finally, in 2015, the Clara Barton's Missing Soldiers Office Museum opened its doors to the public. Operated by the National Museum of Civil War Medicine, this museum showcases Clara Barton's incredible efforts in locating missing soldiers during the Civil War. It offers visitors a glimpse into her life and work.

Today, visitors to the Clara Barton's Missing Soldiers Office Museum can explore the carefully preserved artifacts and documents that tell the story of Clara Barton's selfless dedication to reuniting families torn apart by war. The museum serves as a testament to Clara Barton's unwavering compassion and determination, highlighting her pivotal role in shaping American history.

The discovery of Clara Barton's Missing Soldiers Office and the subsequent establishment of the museum are reminders of the enduring impact of one woman's tireless efforts. Clara Barton's legacy continues to inspire and educate people of all ages about the importance of empathy, resilience, and the power of humanitarian action.

As we reflect on Clara Barton's remarkable journey, let us celebrate her legacy and honor her memory by carrying forward her spirit of compassion and service to others. The Clara Barton's Missing Soldiers Office Museum stands as a lasting tribute to a true American hero whose extraordinary contributions continue to resonate with people around the world.

Portrayals of Clara Barton in Fiction

Clara Barton's remarkable life and legacy have inspired numerous fictional depictions in books, films, and television shows. While these portrayals may take creative liberties, they highlight the enduring impact of Clara Barton's contributions to history.

One fictional work that features Clara Barton is "Numbering All the Bones" by Ann Rinaldi. This historical novel explores Barton's involvement with Andersonville Prison during the Civil War, shedding light on the challenging conditions faced by prisoners and Barton's efforts to provide aid and relief.

Another depiction of Clara Barton can be found in the biographical short film "Angel of Mercy" (1939), directed by Edward L. Cahn. In this film, Sara Haden portrays Barton, and Ann Rutherford plays a woman whose brother's death in a Civil War battle inspires her to join Barton in her humanitarian work.

In the NBC TV series "Voyagers!" (1982–1983), Clara Barton makes an appearance in the episode titled "The Travels of Marco ... and Friends." In this adventurous show about time travel, Phineas Bogg and Jeffrey Jones rescue Barton (played by Patricia Donahue) from a burning wagon. Jeffrey, a young boy from 1982, uses mouth-to-mouth resuscitation (a technique unknown in Barton's time) to save her life, ensuring that she can continue her mission and eventually found the American Red Cross.

More recently, Clara Barton has been portrayed by Mandy Moore in an episode of "Drunk History." This comedic show features a humorous retelling of Barton's accomplishments during and after the Civil War, narrated by Amber Ruffin.

Additionally, Clara Barton appears in the animated film "America: The Motion Picture," where she is voiced by Megan Leahy. Although this portrayal is highly fictionalized, it brings Clara Barton's character into a new light within a comedic and exaggerated setting.

In the HBO series "The Gilded Age" (2022), Clara Barton is portrayed by Linda Emond. This historical drama showcases Barton's involvement during a pivotal era of American history, offering viewers a glimpse into her life and impact.

These fictional depictions of Clara Barton serve to keep her story alive in popular culture and inspire new generations to learn about her remarkable achievements. While they may take creative liberties for entertainment purposes, they ultimately celebrate the enduring legacy of a courageous and compassionate woman whose contributions continue to resonate today. Clara Barton's story reminds us that ordinary individuals can make an extraordinary difference in the world through kindness, determination, and unwavering dedication to helping others.

Remembering a Trailblazer

Clara Barton's impact on American history and humanitarian efforts is commemorated in various ways, ensuring that her legacy continues to inspire and educate people of all ages.

The Clara Barton Homestead, where Barton was born in North Oxford, Massachusetts, is now a museum open to the public. Visitors can explore the place where Barton spent her early years and learn about her remarkable life and achievements.

In 1948, a special stamp was issued featuring a portrait of Clara Barton alongside the symbol of the American Red Cross. This stamp honored Barton's role in founding the Red Cross and her dedication to humanitarian work.

In 1973, Clara Barton was inducted into the National Women's Hall of Fame, recognizing her as a trailblazer for women's rights and her significant contributions to society.

In 1995, Clara Barton was featured on a set of U.S. postage stamps commemorating the Civil War. This recognition highlighted Barton's pivotal role in providing aid to soldiers during the war and her lasting impact on American history.

In 2019, Clara Barton was honored as one of the inaugural members of the Government Executive magazine's Government Hall of Fame. This prestigious recognition celebrated Barton's leadership and contributions to public service.

Exhibits in the National Museum of American History showcase artifacts related to Clara Barton's life and the impact of the American Red Cross. While the Clara Barton Red Cross ambulance was once a signature artifact, it is now part of a rich collection that educates visitors about America's history during times of war.

In the Disney show Sydney to the Max, there is a middle school named after Clara Barton. This portrayal reflects Barton's enduring legacy and her importance as a historical figure.

In 2008, Clara Barton was posthumously inducted into the New Jersey Hall of Fame, recognizing her roots and contributions to the state's history.

These commemorations and tributes ensure that Clara Barton's legacy remains alive in the hearts and minds of people across the nation. From museums and stamps to schools and halls of fame, Clara Barton's enduring influence continues to inspire future generations to serve their communities and strive for positive change.

A Champion for Education

As a young girl, Clara enjoyed reading books and exploring the world around her. However, she soon realized that not all children had the same opportunities to learn and grow.

Clara noticed that many girls in her community did not go to school. Instead, they stayed at home to help with chores or take care of younger siblings. This troubled Clara deeply because she believed that every child should have the chance to receive an education and pursue their dreams.

Determined to make a difference, Clara started talking to families and community leaders about the importance of education. She explained how education could empower children, especially girls, to become confident and independent individuals.

Clara's passion for education led her to take action. She volunteered at local schools, helping children with their studies and encouraging them to dream big. Clara believed that knowledge was the key to unlocking endless possibilities in life.

As Clara grew older, she became even more committed to her mission. She traveled to different towns and villages, speaking to families and urging them to send their children, including girls, to school. She emphasized that education was not just for boys; it was for everyone.

Clara's campaign gained momentum, and soon, many people joined her cause. Together, they raised money to build schools, provide books and supplies, and support children who wanted to learn.

Through her efforts, Clara not only promoted education for all but also inspired others to become advocates for children's rights. She showed that one person's determination and compassion could make a big difference in the lives of many.

As time passed, more and more children, regardless of their background or gender, began attending school. Clara's dream of education for all was slowly becoming a reality.

Today, Clara's legacy lives on through the countless children who have benefited from her efforts. She taught us that education is a powerful tool that can change lives and build brighter futures.

Clara's story reminds us of the importance of promoting education for all. Let's follow in her footsteps by advocating for equal access to education and ensuring that every child has the chance to learn, grow, and fulfill their dreams. Together, we can make a world where education truly is for everyone!

Pioneering Women's Rights

Clara wasn't just any ordinary woman; she was a pioneer, a trailblazer who believed in the power of equality and the importance of women's rights.

Clara grew up in a time when many girls and women didn't have the same opportunities as boys and men. Girls were expected to stay at home and learn household tasks, while boys went to school and pursued careers. But Clara was different. She had a thirst for knowledge and a strong desire to help others.

As Clara grew older, she faced many challenges because of her gender. Despite these obstacles, Clara never gave up. She worked tirelessly to prove that women were just as capable as men. She believed that women deserved the right to education, the right to vote, and the right to pursue their dreams.

One of Clara Barton's most significant contributions to improving women's rights was through her work as a nurse and humanitarian during the American Civil War. When the war broke out, Clara volunteered to help care for wounded soldiers. At that time, nursing was considered a job only for women, but Clara showed that women could excel in this field and make a difference on the battlefield.

Clara's dedication and hard work earned her respect and admiration, not just from the soldiers she cared for but from people all across the country. Her bravery and compassion helped change the perception of women's capabilities.

After the war, Clara continued her mission to advocate for women's rights. She became involved in the suffrage movement, which fought for women's right to vote. Clara believed that women should have a say in important decisions that affected their lives and their country.

Clara Barton's efforts inspired many other women to stand up for their rights. She showed them that they could achieve great things if they were determined and courageous. Clara's legacy continues to inspire girls and women around the world to pursue their dreams and fight for equality.

Clara Barton played a vital role in improving women's rights by breaking barriers, challenging stereotypes, and advocating for equality. She proved that women are capable of anything they set their minds to, and she paved the way for future generations of women to follow in her footsteps. Clara Barton's story teaches us that no dream is too big and no obstacle is too great when you believe in yourself and strive for change.

Lessons from Clara Barton

In the remarkable life of Clara Barton, there are valuable lessons that can inspire and guide us, especially as young individuals. Let's explore some important lessons we can learn from the experiences of this courageous and compassionate woman:

1. Determination in the Face of Challenges:

Clara Barton faced numerous challenges throughout her life, from overcoming shyness as a child to advocating for humanitarian causes in adulthood. Despite these obstacles, she never gave up. Clara teaches us the importance of determination and perseverance when faced with difficulties. No matter how tough things get, keep pushing forward with resilience and belief in yourself.

2. Compassion and Kindness Towards Others:

One of Clara Barton's most defining qualities was her deep compassion for others. During the American Civil War, she tirelessly cared for wounded soldiers, regardless of which side they fought for. Clara's example teaches us the value of showing kindness and empathy towards everyone we encounter. Small acts of kindness can have a big impact on someone's life.

3. Courage to Make a Difference:

Clara Barton was not afraid to step into challenging situations to help those in need.

She risked her safety to provide aid on battlefields and ventured into war-torn areas to assist victims. Clara's courage teaches us that sometimes, making a difference requires bravery and stepping out of our comfort zones. Be brave and stand up for what you believe in, even if it's not easy.

4. Resilience in Adversity:

Throughout her life, Clara Barton encountered setbacks and criticism. Despite these hardships, she remained resilient and focused on her goals. Clara's story reminds us that setbacks are part of life, but we have the power to bounce back stronger. Embrace challenges as opportunities to learn and grow.

5. Advocating for Equality and Justice:

Clara Barton was a pioneer for women's rights and civil rights. She believed in equality for all and fought against discrimination. Clara's advocacy inspires us to stand up against injustice and inequality. Use your voice and actions to promote fairness and inclusivity in your community and beyond.

6. Empowering Others Through Education:

As a teacher, Clara Barton understood the importance of education. She empowered children to learn and grow, advocating for accessible schooling for all. Clara's dedication to education teaches us the transformative power of knowledge. Value education and strive to empower others through learning.

7. Making a Difference, One Person at a Time:

Clara Barton's impactful work started with individual acts of kindness and grew into a nationwide movement. Her story teaches us that even one person can make a significant difference in the world. Never underestimate the impact of your actions, no matter how small they may seem.

Clara Barton's life is a testament to the power of compassion, courage, and determination. Let her inspiring story guide you as you navigate life's challenges and strive to make a positive impact on the world around you. Embrace these lessons from Clara Barton and use them to shape your own journey of growth and service.

ERIC LYLANI

CONCLUSION

As we conclude our exploration of Clara Barton's life and legacy, we are left with an indelible impression of a woman who defied conventions and dedicated herself to serving humanity. Clara's story teaches us invaluable lessons—about perseverance in the face of adversity, compassion for those in need, and the profound impact one individual can have on the world.

Through Clara's unwavering commitment to education, healthcare, and humanitarianism, she laid the groundwork for modern philanthropy and disaster relief. Her founding of the American Red Cross continues to save lives and alleviate suffering around the globe.

But Clara's impact extends beyond organizations and institutions; it resides in the hearts of those inspired by her example. Her courage in the midst of chaos, her determination to overcome obstacles, and her empathy for the vulnerable serve as a beacon for us all.

As we reflect on Clara Barton's enduring legacy, let us honor her by embracing her principles in our own lives. May we continue her legacy of compassion, resilience, and service to others. Let us remember Clara Barton not only as a historical figure but as a timeless symbol of humanity at its best.

Thank you for joining me on this journey through Clara Barton's extraordinary life.

May her story continue to inspire and uplift us, reminding us of the difference one person can make when driven by compassion and conviction.

Made in the USA
Middletown, DE
01 December 2024

65831770R00060